When God Calls A Writer

Moving Past Insecurity

to

Write with Confidence

By Deanne Welsh

Keep writing!

Deanne Welsh

Cover Design by Janet Hirata Stall
www.JanetHirataStall.com

Scripture quotations marked (MSG) are taken from The Message, Copyright ©1993, 1994, 1995, 1996, 2000, 2001, 2002 by Eugene H. Peterson.

Unstoppable Writers books are available at special discounts when purchased in bulk for premiums and sales promotions as well as for fund-raising or educational use. Special editions or book excerpts can also be created to specification. For details, contact **WritingFreedom@deannewelsh.com**.

Unstoppable Writers Publishing
www.UnstoppableWriters.com

For every writer
trusting God and the process
of painting pictures with their pen.

For every reader
changed by the courage of a writer
and the power of a single sentence or idea.

Acknowledgements

It takes a village to write a book and I am eternally grateful for my village.

Thank you to my parents who believed in my writing, even when it was full of spelling errors and 2nd grade fantasies.

The **Unstoppable Writers community** inspired me to pen this message and start a revolution of writers serving a greater purpose while catapulting one another to success. They are my inspiration.

A special thanks to my team of readers who gave me invaluable feedback: Joel Penhallegon, Angie Elliston, Jennifer Lindsay, Teresa Colon, Sharon Martinez and Ruth Deaton. I could not have hit publish without you.

Table of Contents

INTRODUCTION

We question it, the burning desire within us to write. Am I kidding myself?

Yet the burning desire persists. It begins as a nudge to pick up a pen and put words on paper. Ignoring it fuels the flame, pushing it deeper and wider into our souls.

Have you felt the call?

To put words on paper and bring ideas to life. If you question your desire to write, you are not alone.

Every writer begins as Moses did, standing before a burning bush while questioning our qualifications, abilities, and influence.

We argue with God and ourselves. Am I crazy to write? Is this a fool's errand?

The truth is that you have been called, by name, to bring life, freedom, and healing through the message, stories, pictures, and words God has entrusted to you.

It's time to learn how to remove barricades of insecurity and write with confidence through the call and transformation of Moses.

Jot a note here of when you first felt the nudge to write:

THE CALL

The Call of Moses

"Moses. Moses."

God called Moses specifically, by name, just as He calls you (Exodus 3:4).

Your desire to write is a gift from God.

Because writing is one of our greatest gifts, Satan is bent on keeping us silent, distracted and stagnant. As soon as Moses received the call, his personal dragon-lies and insecurities moved in to cast doubt (Exodus 4:10-13).

We face the blank page with fear. We lack the audacity to call ourselves a writer. The process of writing and finishing projects is daunting.

The trip back to Egypt, then out of Egypt, and to the Promised Land is long.

Where do I start? What shall I write about? What if my words are not good enough? What if no one cares? Am I really meant to write?

Your desire to write reveals you were designed to write.

Like Moses, we have questions and dragon-lies that hold us back.

What's holding you back from pursuing your calling? Write it down:

Who am I? Why me?

When called, our focus immediately shifts to ourselves. If we are not careful, we spiral into self-doubt and internal speculation, *I'm not good enough. I don't think I have what it takes* (Exodus 3:11).

God's firm reminder is to look to Him, "I am with you."

We do not write alone.

Just as the disciples only saw a few fish and loaves, and Peter stared at the unsupportive waves, our tendency is to focus on perceived limited resources and the task instead of the One calling us.

Pause for two minutes and focus upward, on the One calling you to write.

Brainstorm a list of His characteristics and qualifications here:

Who is sending me?

Think about your favorite place in nature. Look around. The designer of every leaf, flower, and creature is the One who is calling you and has promised to be with you.

God is an artist; your art connects you powerfully and intimately to Him.

He is "I-AM-WHO-I-AM. (Exodus 3:14)"

You don't need to rely on your own skills and resources. Write a prayer of thanks to God for providing all you need today and to fulfill your calling:

What if the people do not believe?

We want to see results now. What if no one reads my writing? What if I don't receive a book contract? What if I cannot make an income from my words?

Faith.

Although we want to know the exact results and fixed destination, God knows that this would stunt our growth.

Trust.

God is working on our behalf and for our good. This could mean a best-seller or a small but intimate group of readers.

We want guarantees and God asks us to step out in faith. To begin writing and to trust Him with the process.

Thankfully He does provide encouragement for us along the way: positive feedback, a supportive writing group, words in a book confirming your calling...

Write down three of the signs God has already given you regarding your calling as a writer:

What if I don't speak or write well enough?

"And who do you think made the human mouth? And who makes some mute, some deaf, some sighted, some blind? Isn't it I, God? So, get going. I'll be right there with you – with your mouth! I'll be right there to teach you what to say."
Exodus 4:11-12, MSG

We don't have to figure out our book marketing plan or exact audience building strategy when we begin. God will provide and teach.

Opportunities, mentors, books, resources, and articles… He will bring them to you at the right time.

Start today.

Decide what starting today will look like. Write it down here so you can come back whenever you need a reminder:

The Responsibility Dodge

He [Moses] said, "Oh, Master, please! Send somebody else!"
Exodus 4:13, MSG

Although we often delay God's work through procrastination and distractibility, He is too kind to allow us to miss the adventure.

Imagine if God had told Moses, "You're right. Go back to tending sheep. I should have picked someone else."

Would Moses have been content tending sheep?

Even as a young man, Moses had a burning desire to see his people free. His desire without God led to the death of an Egyptian after which he escaped to the desert. In his mind, his hope of freeing the Israelites was lost. Meanwhile God was preparing Moses to lead Israel.

Where Moses saw lack, God saw power and provision. Every single day tending sheep, Moses was being equipped to lead Israel to freedom. Regardless of the profession you're coming from, trust that God has prepared you and will continue to provide for you as you write, speak, and create.

You are ready, right now, to begin.

"The reality is that the Lord never calls the qualified; He qualifies the called."

Henry Blackaby

Get all your doubts and questions out on paper. Write a bullet list of your fears, dragon-lies, and insecurities below.

Then prayerfully release them to God and say," Yes, I am willing to write and do the work to become the writer you are calling me to be."

The Call to Write

When God nudges you to write, you may not feel ready or worthy. You may wonder if you are enough or have enough to begin. You may feel unprepared and struggle with procrastination.

It's normal to struggle with where to start or be plagued by fear and insecurity.

God understands the courage required to trust Him and the process of writing.

He places internal and external burning bushes in our lives to confirm His calling.

Your desire to write is a burning bush within you. Your dreams of serving a greater purpose and making an impact is a burning bush. The ideas, stories, and specific wording that keep you up at night are burning bushes showing you the path forward.

When books, articles and mentors appear at the right time, they are burning bushes pointing you forward. When someone admires your wording, allow their encouragement to be a burning bush showing you the way.

Instead of belittling your ability and knowledge, thank Him for the gift of writing, humbly submit, surrender your gift, and the writing journey to Him, "*Father, give me the courage to write and speak. Show me the way forward.*"

You have a gift from God, but you need to know that there is an enemy who wants to keep you silent, hiding, and feeling small or insignificant.

Don't be surprised if after accepting and surrendering your gift, a wave of opposition arises. The liar, that great dragon, will begin his taunts trying to derail you, "*You don't have what it takes. You will never be heard. Your story does not matter. Others are writing and speaking better than you. You are not needed...*"

Don't listen.

Whether the Dragon comes to your mind with negative thoughts or through people who lack vision, don't listen.

You must believe in God's call, in the burning bushes, and in the message or story God is giving you.

There are specific people who need your story and words. You have wording, pictures, and stories that will speak to specific people as no one else's will.

Whether God gives you an audience of two or of thousands, trust His call and do everything in your power to follow with excellence, persistence and courage.

Whether God calls you to write full time, or write as a hobby, trust Him in the process of discovery.

Will you follow Him with your gift and desire to write?

Write a short declaration of your intention and date it:

Your "yes" changes everything.

Just as Moses left the familiar life of shepherding to walk back into Egypt, embracing the writing life will mean transformation.

It begins with you, but only by looking to Him.

Although awe fills us as we look at Moses, his power and purpose came from God.

If we try to figure it out on our own, it will take us years. If we look to God, it may still take years, but each year will bring movement and a deeper connection to God and the ministry-work He is calling us to.

Ministry-work. Each ministry takes work. Our work is an opportunity for ministry. Writing is no different.

God provides the power, provision, and people.

We bring humility, trust, and openness to receive His Word and guidance. God does the miraculous. We bring a mustard seed of faith.

This is the time of crossing over and stepping into your calling and new identity.

You are a writer.

Say it aloud.

Start introducing yourself to others as a writer.

There is no secret threshold to cross before calling yourself a writer. It's not when your first book is published, or when others think you are a writer.

Have you decided to write with the gift God has given you? If you answer yes, you are a writer.

Whether this is your first or ten thousandth time surrendering your writing to Him, take a moment to do that here.

Remember this moment and repeat it often.

Now that we have determined God's call to write and your response to His call, where to begin?

We start small, with who and where we are.

Accepting His call to write is accepting the cloak of responsibility.

This is not the time for excuses and half-hearted attempts or returning to the vomit of doubt and self-obsession.

This is the time to look to Him.

GOD'S WRITER

Face-to-Face Connection

"I am the vine, you are the branches. When you are joined with me and I with you, and the relation is intimate and organic, the harvest is sure to be abundant."
John 15:5, MSG

If you were hired for a company and introduced to your manager, you would not go weeks on end without checking in with them.

You would look to them for guidance on your training, priorities, and projects.

Why do we think God does not care about our creativity and words?

Look at a tree. Look to the sky.

He created it, is an Artist, and delights in bringing order, simplicity, and stunning beauty to chaos.

There is a reason we feel fully alive and deeply connected when we create and long to create despite dragons, obstacles and constraints. We can trust Him with the mess of ourselves and ideas. He wants all of us and our art.

Moses followed God into and out of Egypt. He met with God despite complaining followers, hunger, and a forty-year detour in the desert.

Although we hope that our writing is met with instant success, are we willing to continue for forty years in the desert if this is where God leads?

Although we hope to change the lives of millions, are we willing to be invisible to the world except for the handful of followers God gives us?

The journey of faith is simple. One step.

Then another.

The writing life is simple. One word.

Then another.

Although we do not know what our pen will uncover, or where the road leads, we can know that the Creator is with us.

We can trust Him, even when we struggle to have confidence in ourselves and our words.

We and our writing are His.

God Writes

Instead of wondering what God thinks, read His Word.

It continues to be a best-seller.

Read it for your heart, mind, life and writing.

Did you know?

- A father swore to give the first thing that greeted him on arriving home to God, only to find out it was his most beloved only child?

- God opened both the eyes and mouth of a donkey to rebuke his master.

- God has a special place in His heart for David, the poet warrior king, despite his failure?

- The Bible is full of romance novel material: true love, lust, greed, deceit, adultery, and redemption?

- The Bible contains poetry, prose, stories, history, wisdom, and parables.

If we allow it to, the Bible will point us towards life and freedom through stories and word pictures.

It can be first thing in the morning, a lunch break thing, or last thing before falling asleep.

Journal and paint pictures as you read.

Allow His artist words to inspire your artist heart and slay the dragon-lies hounding you.

He is the one who calls, defines, and gives us our worth as writers.

As we move to hearing God speak, ensure that what you hear always lines up with his Word. His written Word is the compass to ensure we are not heading into the woods and are staying true to His path and calling.

Start reading the Bible today. Start small.

Pick a book of the Bible, or a study to help you along. Better yet, find a friend to do it with.

Pick a time to do it and write it below:

God Speaks

We are taught to pray in church, but how often are we taught to listen?

Instead of struggling with how or what to pray, ask God, *what should I pray for?*

Begin by pouring out your heart to Him. No matter is too small or unimportant to Him.

My help and glory are in God
--granite-strength and safe-harbor-God –
So trust him absolutely, people;
lay your lives on the line for him.
God is a safe place to be.

Psalm 62:8, MSG

Just as a toddler has absolute faith that his parents will care about the cookie he wants or the bruise on his knee, nothing is too small to bring to God.

What's on your heart today?

Every Hour, Every Day by Anne Golias Peterson

I know you're always listening, God,
no matter when I call.
You never miss a single thing,
like when a sparrow falls.
You understand my feelings
and you never back away.
And that is why I need you —
every hour, every day.

Restorative Writing & Listening Prayer

Each morning, I open my fifty-cent composition book and begin to free-write. No editing. No judging.

Most of my entries begin with, "A new day has begun," or, "Another day..."

My emotions, thoughts, experiences, and questions all find their way to the page. If I'm struggling to think clearly, "*I feel foggy brained and out of it today...*" or honest confessions, "*I don't know what I'm doing.*"

When my mind stops scurrying and I am done getting my thoughts onto the paper, I pause.

Taking a few deep breaths to quiet my thoughts, I whisper "*I am ready to hear from you.*"

The three questions I continually return to are:

- *Father God, what do you say?*
- *Jesus, what do you say?*
- *Holy Spirit, what do you say?*

I write one of these questions on the top of a new page. After asking a question, I close my eyes and wait.

As I sit in silence, I pay attention to the words, pictures and verses that come to mind.

I write my name and then begin transcribing the pictures and words. Although I was raised in the church, I never thought God would want direct and daily communication with me. It takes courage and faith to trust that He wants such a deep and meaningful connection to me. Yet I have only to look at Jesus to see that it is true.

In the year since beginning this practice of listening prayer and restorative writing, I have been transformed.

This book is the result of listening prayer and restorative writing.

He has given me the courage to write, start online writing retreats, and serve in a deeper and more significant way than I would have chosen on my own.

He has catapulted me to connections and opportunities I previously withdrew and hid from.

He has unleashed my voice when it was under an invisible weight of silence, self-hatred, and never feeling good enough.

As you write, pray, and listen, I know He will do the same for you.

Your calling and ministry will look different than mine because each person is called to a specific and unique role; but as you listen, He will guide. On the next page is an example of the words God placed on my heart as I paused and listened to Him.

Dearest,

You are valued.

I will reveal and speak...not always before you move forward but know that even the deepest disappointment and failures you face are opportunities.

I am the most creatively-saturated being. I create life from the void, something from nothing.

I speak every language and know every heart. I know the stories and experiences that will allow people to see and hear. I interpret even the wrongly worded and use even the most broken and shattered of vessels for my glory.

You can always rely on me when I say "go" or "stop." You can trust my guidance every single time. I will make a way through the sea and calm the storm. I turn situations around in the blink of an eye.

Communication with me is never wasted: requests, gratitude, lament... Being close to me is the safest place to be.

Never be too busy to stop and listen to me. This is what Martin Luther knew when he said he would spend even more time praying on his busiest days.

You can trust me, Jesus.

Now it's your turn:

Physical Space

Live in me. Make your home in me just as I do in you. In the same way that a branch can't bear grapes by itself but only by being joined to the vine, you can't bear fruit unless you are joined to me…But if you make your home with me and my words are at home in you, you can be sure that whatever you ask will be listened to and acted upon.

John 15:4, 5-8

As God speaks, I have found it helpful to keep physical reminders and notes in view around my home.

When dragon-lies attack, these reminders keep me connected to God and seeking His truth.

They fuel my inspiration, courage and resilience.

You can post notecards, pictures, or art around your home as mental triggers to trust, pray, and rely on Him.

Are there reminders around your home of God's truth and goodness?

What is He teaching you today? Write the verse or lesson down on a notecard and display it prominently.

When people talk about spending time with God, I don't see it as a separate thing. He's always with me.

Anne Golias Peterson

He is with you every moment.

Right now, as you sit reading this chapter.

Pause for a moment and ask Him, *what do You have for me today?*

Don't be Afraid

When God calls, He does not ask us to part the waters or provide manna. He asks for trust and actions fueled by faith. When God calls, He provides the power and:

- Removes obstacles
- Loosens your voice
- Sets burning bushes within and around you to spur you forward
- Sends help
- Calls you by name
- Fuels your pen
- Provides ideas
- Heals you
- Equips you in tangible and invisible ways

If you are finding it difficult to look beyond the small fishes and loaves in your hand, don't be afraid. God makes something out of nothing, speaking the world into Creation. His Word is Christ.

He is passionate about language, communicating, pictures, and stories.

You have little. I can work with that.
You are unschooled. I can teach you.
You are foolish. I am wisdom.
You are overwhelmed. I am peace.
You are stuck. I am unstoppable.

One Requirement

Our only job is to listen and follow.

God is the one who paints pictures in our minds and plants stories in our souls, so we can share them and paint them for others.

He is the source of abundant creativity.

I am the Vine, you are the branches. When you're joined with me and I with you, the relation is intimate and organic, the harvest is sure to be abundant.

John 15:5

Your creativity connects you to God.

Don't be afraid.

Trust.

The Spirit of Your Calling

"The Spirit of God, the Master, is on me because God anointed me. He sent me to preach good news to the poor, heal the heartbroken, announce freedom to all captives, pardon all prisoners.

God sent me to announce the year of his grace — a celebration of God's destruction of our enemies — and to comfort all who mourn...Messages of joy instead of news of doom, a praising heart instead of a languid spirit.

Rename them "Oaks of Righteousness" planted by God to display his glory. They rebuild the old ruins, raise a new city out of the wreckage."

Excerpts from Isaiah 61, MSG

Your words have power.

This does not mean that we only write happy pieces. As we embrace both the devastation and celebration of life, we bring hope and light to our readers. They are not alone.

Will you use your gift, regardless of the genre of your writing, to bring freedom and light?

Write a list of the gifts you want to give your readers here:

YOUR SERVICE

Your Ministry-Work

As you move forward in your writing-work-ministry, ask God.

- *Who are you calling me to?*
- *What are they facing and struggling with?*
- *What do they need and desire?*
- *What is the message you have for them?*
- *How can I bring freedom and serve them?*

Moses was called to the enslaved Israelites who were oppressed and taken advantage of. They needed a leader to guide them to freedom, to a place of their own, and toward a renewed connection to God.

The message of Moses was the promise of a new life as the old life was left behind. He stayed attuned to the people while keeping his eyes and heart fixed on God.

When problems, hunger, and complaints arose, Moses went to God for solutions.

Although Moses did not enter the Promised Land, I imagine him watching the Israelites from the mountaintop and being filled with peace and thanksgiving over God's faithfulness.

Moses fulfilled his calling, faithfully shepherding the people God gave him, through trials and with face-to-face communication with God.

Although it is easy to get stuck on the failure of Moses, he was faithful even after failure. God knew that Moses was the leader the Israelites needed during their crossing over out of slavery into freedom, and during their years of wandering in the desert.

Responding to God's call does not guarantee worldly success.

Responding to God's call does guarantee a deeper connection to Him and His people.

Are you ready to agree to serve Him fully and faithfully with your gift of writing, regardless of the outcome?

Are you ready to take opportunities even if they are out of your comfort zone?

Are you ready to learn how to lead?

If you answered yes, look for opportunities to learn about leadership and practice leading. Whether in your community, church, or home.

The following questions will become the cornerstones of your ministry-work.

1) Your Audience: *Who are you calling me to serve?*

2) Their Pain: *What are they struggling with?*

3) Their Pleasure: *What do they need or desire?*

4) The Message: *What are they saying? What is the message you have for them? How can I write it in a way they will understand and relate to?*

5) Your Service: *How can I help and serve my audience?*

The good news is that your ministry-work is not about you.

Although we all know the name of Moses, his ministry-work was focused on the Israelites and their freedom.

The journey of faith and writing are simple: begin with God and ask Him to show you the people He is calling you to serve.

Brainstorm your answers here. They may change over time. This is normal. As we mature and move forward, our clarity increases.

1) Your Audience:

2) Their Pain:

3) Their Pleasure:

4) The Message (God has for them & what they are saying):

5) Your Service:

Get Specific

As we serve the people God is entrusting to us, the needs and desires can be overwhelming.

It does not have to be.

Just as the journey of faith and writing are simple. A single step leads to the next.

When it comes to your audience, focus on one specific problem at a time.

Solve one specific problem for them. Then move on to the next.

As you focus on your people and pray for them, you will fall in love with them. These are the people God has given you to serve. You connect to them through the message, voice and ministry-work God has given you.

Moses tried to do the work on his own and it ended in the death of an Egyptian and Moses' desertion to the desert.

Don't try to go it alone.

Invite God into your writing journey. Ask Him to guide you to help in the form of a friend, writing group, accountability partner or writing coach.

There will be seasons where God calls you to Himself alone and others when He provides people to walk with you.

Regardless of the season He is calling you to, you can trust Him.

What season are you in? Who is He providing as a help?

What if I don't know who God is calling me to serve?

If you are struggling to hear the answers as to who your audience is, start with these questions instead.

- *What did you create me for?*
- *What is my purpose?*
- *What are my strengths?*
- *What are my weaknesses?*
- *What am I passionate about?*
- *What has been life-changing for me?*
- *Who have I helped in the past?*
- *Who can I help in the future?*
- *How can I help them?*

Don't be discouraged if the answers do not emerge immediately. Keep asking. Ask friends, hire a coach or spiritual adviser to discern with you, and keep asking your Creator.

Post this verse as a daily reminder to keep asking.

For everyone who asks and keeps on asking receives; and he who seeks and keeps on seeking finds; and to him who knocks and keeps on knocking, the door shall be opened.

Luke 11:10

Persistence is a super-power.

Challenges

The Israelites were hungry, discouraged, and even forgot God in the desert.

Challenges are a part of life. Don't take them personally.

They say nothing about your potential as a writer or your worth as a person.

While the results are in God's hands, He has given us control over our attitude, effort, response, and actions.

Upon facing a challenge, we choose whether to give up or keep going.

When confronted with failure, whisper this prayer,

> God, help me persist:
> I am willing to do the work
> to become a better writer.

God provides inspiration, words, and opportunities.

The only way to carry the heavy cloak of responsibility is to stay connected to Him and allow Him to carry the weight of it.

"So be content with who you are, and don't put on airs. God's strong hand is on you; he'll promote you at the right time. Live carefree before God; he is most careful with you."

1 Peter 5:7, MSG

Thinking or trying harder will not fix your problems. Obsessing over them will result in heightened anxiety and burn-out, both of which are poison to creativity.

When a problem arises, look up.

Affirm your trust in Him and wait to see what He will do.

If your mind is spinning, try a breath prayer to steady your thoughts on Him.

As you breathe in for three counts, say one of the names of God in your mind: Jesus, Holy Spirit, Comforter...

Pause for a moment before breathing out and silently speaking a centering phrase: bring your peace, heal my heart, carry this burden, show me your light...

Challenges are an opportunity to deepen our connection to God and others.

Call a safe and God-connected friend. Ask them to pray with you. Pour out your heart to them. We were created to share our burdens.

Who are the safe friends you can call about your writing? Write their names on the next page and don't be afraid to reach out.

If you don't have these type of friends, ask God to make you this type of friend and to bring them into your life.

Changes

As we follow God's call, a process of releasing and receiving is set in motion.

Moses left behind his flock of sheep and his home of forty years. He left behind the identity, responsibility, and security he was accustomed to.

He walked into a new responsibility, a new flock of people, and new challenges.

Although he was still Moses, the transition required exponential trust and an open-handedness to let go and receive what God had for him.

As you move forward in your writing journey, you will face challenges and growth opportunities to step up to God's call.

As you move forward, prayerfully ask:

- Who do I need to become to fulfill this calling?
- Who can help me as I move forward?
- What is my next step?

Journal your responses below:

Truth Transformation

The truth will set you free, but only if you embrace it and allow yourself to be shaped and changed by it.

We walk into the light that we may be illuminated and transformed.

Just as a caterpillar enters a season of darkness and safety as it grows into a bold bright butterfly, we need safe spaces and people to develop our voice and writing.

When we stop feeling threatened and destroyed by feedback, we can begin learning from it. Kind yet truthful mentors are needed.

Feedback is an opportunity, not the final word on our worth.

At the age of twelve, I allowed the disappointment of not making the volleyball team to dictate my reality and reaction. I quit playing, *What's the point? I'm a failure at volleyball.*

My failure had the final word, because I allowed it to.

Disregarding my passion and joy for playing, I took the feedback I received as the final judgement on my potential as a player. It took over 10 years for me to realize I had a different choice available.

Instead of giving up, I could have persisted and allowed the failure to fuel my passion instead of extinguishing it. If I had focused on practicing and improving every day, I could have made the team the following year.

Feedback is a stepping stone to success. It is not a death threat unless we allow ourselves to be intimated and invalidated by it.

Feedback is what you make of it.

Journal below, how will you embrace feedback?

Uncomfortable

The Israelites had been in Egypt for centuries. What would life look like if they left?

It was uncomfortable for Moses to walk away from a life of certainty and familiarity, even though he desired more than to herd sheep.

When God calls a writer, He is calling us to move into the discomfort of change and transformation.

He is calling us toward vulnerability and community.

Be kind to yourself as you walk into new and uncharted territory.

Don't buy into the poison of comparison, believing that some people were born writing well and feeling comfortable speaking in front of others.

Every single person you see with success has walked through seasons of discomfort.

No one is born with everything figured out.

Don't be afraid.

God is with you and will guide you through the waters, through the desert and toward the fulfillment of His calling on your life.

You don't have to strive or make it happen. Trust and seek Him. Lean on Him for direction, answers, and opportunities.

He desires to carry the weight of your projects and writing career.

Will you trust Him enough to take the next step?

Are you experiencing discomfort and growth?

Take a moment to journal about the discomfort you are experiencing and the rewards and growth it is leading you toward.

As you pray and process:

- Surrender these areas to God
- Ask Him for specific help and to open your eyes to identify the help when it appears.

Moving Forward

You are called by God to write.

Your writing and creativity connects you to the heart of God.

We can trust Him with ourselves and writing, even if the process is uncomfortable.

There are benefits and rewards when we write.

We can become like trusting children, playfully creating with our words and enjoying the process, lost in powerful ideas and stories coming to life.

Now it's time to decide who you will be on this writing journey.

Take a moment to jot down the characteristics you want to embody on your writing journey. Who will you be as a writer?

UNSTOPPABLE WRITERS

Unstoppable Writers are Passionate

Your desire and passion to write are a burning bush from God.

Passion can wax and wane.

To protect and fuel your passion, you must pay attention to it.

- What fuels your passion?
- What dissipates your passion?

Self-care is wrapped up with our passion. When we are burnt out, our passion becomes listless and pale.

When we are taking excellent care of ourselves, our passion bursts powerfully into every area of our lives.

- How are you taking care of yourself: body, mind and soul?
- Do you take time to disconnect and rest each week?

Just as fire needs oxygen, your passion needs attention to grow and flourish. Passion is where your journey begins, continues, and ends.

Passion is the fuel to spur you towards greater productivity and persistence.

Rate yourself on a scale of one to ten. How well are you taking care of yourself and your passion?

Brainstorm a list of ways to continue or improve your self-care:

Unstoppable Writers are Productive

We are called to speak up.

Whether in writing or spoken words: it is time to find our voice and the message God is entrusting to us.

We discover these through writing. Lots of writing.

Whether you journal, blog, or work on projects: write every day. Scrawling a few rushed notes on a napkin during your lunch break counts.

Regardless of whether you write poetry, fiction, or nonfiction, you get to decide: will you approach the task of writing consistently and productively?

Don't let dragon-lies burden you with perfectionism or distract you with procrastination.

Today is the day to write.

Moses was called from shepherding sheep — which is typically mundane and boring — to leading a nation out of Egypt. He was quick to find out that leading people was not that different from herding sheep, who can also be stubborn and difficult to direct.

Writing is glorious and mundane.

Show up anyway.

The easiest ways to show up are to know:

- Where you will write?
- When you will write?
- What you will write?

Schedule it.

If it's not scheduled, nothing will get done.

I only write when inspiration strikes. Fortunately, it strikes at nine every morning.

William Faulkner

If God is calling us to write, why not treat it as a non-negotiable vocation?

If you were hired to build a house for someone by a certain date, you would schedule the time for it, ensure you have the resources needed, and hire help to complete the job if necessary.

Instead of treating our writing like a haphazard hobby, what would it look like to treat it as a vocation we are called to?

Would we write more often?

Would we intentionally invest in our craft and its improvement?

Would we set aside a physical space and a time space to write?
It all begins with believing God has called us to write.

Whether we write part-time, full-time, or crammed in the middle of a busy life with children-time, the point is to treat our writing as important enough for space on the calendar.

Don't be discouraged if you are in a season with little available space. Use the little you have with faithful focus.

Many writers began with a few minutes or an hour snatched in the early morning or after the kids were in bed. You are in good company.

Writing consistently will:

- Give you clarity.
- Build your confidence.
- Improve your craft.
- Catapult you forward.

When we go public consistently with our writing, we build trust with others. As we treat ourselves as writers and respect our writing, others will begin to as well.

It begins with the writer.

The Writing Path

Where do I begin?

There are two problems a beginning writer faces:

- Too many ideas.
- No idea of where to begin.

If you are unsure where to begin, find writing prompts or a community to help you.

If you have too many ideas, make a long list and pick one to begin with. I call my long idea list my squirrel list and only focus on one at a time.

As you write, you are not only building trust with your audience, but with yourself.

Will you:

- Write consistently?

- Finish what you begin?

Do everything in your power to answer YES to these questions. This is how you increase your confidence and welcome writing opportunities.

Unstoppable Writers are Persistent

We are called to stand up.

There are countless obstacles that will try to push us down: technical problems, an unsubscribe from our list, a family member wondering why anyone would listen to us: the list is long and personalized to each of us.

When we are faced with a barrier or challenge, we have a choice.

Stay down or stand up.

When God calls a writer, He is with us, but there are still giants to face, waters to walk through and hunger pangs.

Our writing journey is winding and messy. There are green pastures but there are also valleys of the shadow of death.

We have a vision of the future, but we have never walked this way before.

It takes faith, and faith is lived out through persistence.

Persistence is for the present.

How will we respond in this moment?

When you face a challenge, it's okay to break-down, cry, and call a friend. It's okay to put your pen down for day and get a good night sleep.

But don't give up.

Persistence is moving, asking, praying, and believing a way will be made for your writing.

This is not about chasing a dream.

This is about committing yourself to writing, come what may.

The moment you begin to view your persistence as the greatest measure of your success, you begin to celebrate and enjoy the writing journey, one word and book at a time.

This is your Mount Everest.

Writing despite obstacles.

Persistence is a muscle and skill. It can be developed and strengthened with practice.

Draw a line down the center of this page. On the left side make a list of the obstacles you are facing or think you will face. On the right side brainstorm a list of way to overcome them.

Every barrier is an opportunity for a breakthrough.

Here are five ways to move forward:

- Ask God to give you creative ways to overcome whatever is holding you back. Affirm your trust in Him and be on the lookout for His answers.

- Ask specific people for help: accountability, encouragement, expertise etc.

- Read the stories of those who have overcome the obstacles you have faced. Search online or ask an online writing group for recommendations.

- Take yourself on an artist date with no agenda except to nurture and tap into your creativity. It can be a hike, a trip to the museum, or a walk down the street. Often the answers and strength we need emerges when we least expect them to.

- Create mental triggers around your home. These can be art, quotes on notecards, or a vision board. The goal is for them to remind you of why you write and to bolster your courage and faith.

Writing is a learning process.

Is the value, insight, clarity, and character you gain from writing enough to sustain you?

Every writer known for their persistence has answered, *yes.*

Unstoppable Writers are Connected

We are called to serve up.

Although we benefit from our writing, it is not for us.

Our writing connects us to others.

Although writing is a solitary task, it does not have to be lonely. Our writing thrives when our connections are thriving.

We gain feedback, insight, and emotional energy from those around us.

If you are feeling lonely and disconnected on your writing journey, here are five ideas to begin connecting to others:

- Join an in-person or online writing community.
- Find an accountability partner for mutually beneficial feedback and insight.
- Hire a consultant or coach to teach, equip, and help you.
- Take a class on writing.
- As you gain experience and expertise, reach out to aspiring writers and offer your help.

We were not meant to live or write alone.

When we write and live generously, we serve those around us.

God calls us into community.

When He calls a writer, He is calling them to connect.

Instead of thinking you have nothing of value to share or no influence, allow God to open your eyes to your power.

The power of your:

- Pen.
- Life.
- Friendship.

In calling you to be a writer, God is calling you to speak and serve.

Whether your writing is to comfort those who are hurting or to serve as a catalyst for change, God is always on the look out for those willing and ready to serve with their writing.

Whether He calls you to write Christian or secular works of art, He is calling you to serve with excellence.

If you think your influence only begins when you are published, you are missing the thousands of opportunities to influence and connect today, right where you are.

As you write and speak with confidence, others are inspired to do the same.

As you embrace your own story and voice, you create space for the voices and stories of others.

As you nurture a growth-mindset instead of a win-fail mindset, you remind others that failure is a stepping stone and not the end of their story.

God has called you to write. He has also called you to lead. Leadership can happen from behind a written page or from a stage. He will guide you.

Are you willing to serve as a comforter and catalyst to the people God has placed in your life?

Are you willing to lead?

Create Your Village

It takes a village to write a book. Simply look at the acknowledgement section and dedication of any book.

As you write, serve, and lead, don't be afraid to ask for help.

Help is often a simple request away.

We are only as strong as our connection to God and our connections to others.

Even Jesus had a close-knit group of friends he intentionally spent time with. The Trinity is deeply connected to one another.

Who will you connect with on your writing journey?

Brainstorm a list of people you know or wish you knew.

Instead of seeing other writers as competitors, see them as cohorts and co-creators:

- There is room at the table.

- There are plenty of readers available.

- There is no need to compete with one another.

Instead of competing with a win-lose mindset, know that there is room for every single writer to win.

Focus on the writing God has called you to do.

Do your best work and as you grow your best will continue to improve.

Writers need the encouragement, feedback, and ideas of other writers.

Instead of showing up online and at conferences vying for the best position, wondering what people think of you:

- Ask questions.
- Give compliments.
- Encourage.
- Share resources.
- Applaud effort.
- Offer feedback when asked: graciously and gently.

The age of artist wars has passed.

The age of collaboration and connection has begun.

Who will you collaborate and connect with?

Keep adding to your list and do not be afraid to send an email, a note in the mail, or to invite someone for coffee over Skype.

Who will you connect with *this week?*

Unstoppable Writers are Humble

Leadership is never a call to pride or dictatorship.

Jesus offered invitations and opportunities, but never forced a follower.

As we walk with quiet bravery, God expands our influence. People are drawn to the attentive, kind and faithful leader. The leader who accepts responsibility and leads by example.

We don't know it all and never will.

Even those skilled at writing, coaching, or speaking, have more to learn.

Wisdom calls from the street.

Wisdom surrounds us, but we will miss it if we do not ask God to give us new eyes and ears.

This prayer demands honesty about where we are and humility to accept the help of God and others.

We cannot fulfil our calling alone.

Unstoppable Writers are dependent on God and confident in Him and His calling.

We never stop learning and never stop serving.

God is looking for leaders who trust Him enough to do that which feels counter-intuitive and out of our league.

He is looking for writers who trust Him every step, and every word, of the way.

Take a moment to write a prayer of dependence and trust to God.

Unstoppable Writers are Grateful

We do not deserve the call to write, or the gift of writing.

Each breathe is a gift. The strength to write is a gift. The desire to write is a gift.

There will always be a gap between our vision and our current work: humility trusts God with the gap and gratitude thanks Him for His provision, even before it appears.

Gratitude embraces the adventure and basks in small gifts: a quiet hour, words flowing quickly, or an idea cracking open a barrier and pushing us to a breakthrough.

We are most creative when we are relaxed, playful and trusting.

If you don't have a gratitude journal yet, it's time to start one. Write two things a day and soon you won't be able to stop at two.

Gifts surround us, if only we have the eyes and hearts to see and receive them. If you struggle to do so, you are not alone. Know that you can develop gratitude muscles and change the wiring in your brain through practicing gratitude.

What are two things you are thankful for today:

Your Next Steps

The next step God calls us to is often simple:

- Write today.
- Ask another individual for help and support.
- Show up in a Facebook group to encourage or ask for help.
- Send an email.

The humble writer embraces the simplicity of God's call instead of wondering why it is not a grandeur one. General Naaman allowed his pride to hinder his healing. If his servant had not intervened, Naaman would have remained ill instead of following the directions Elisha the prophet sent to him.

His [Naaman] servants caught up with him and said, "Father, if the prophet had asked you to do something hard and heroic, wouldn't you have done it? So why not this simple 'wash and be clean'?

2 Kings 5:13, MSG

What are the simple steps God is calling you to today?

The Rewards of Writing

Although this book has focused on God's burning
bushes calling us to write and the barriers keeping us
from writing, there are great rewards for writers who
consistently pick up their pens.

The flow of creating, the insights gained, and the
contentment of doing what we were created to, are just
the beginning.

There are visible gifts:
- Completed books.
- Thankful readers.
- Career opportunities.
- Income.
- Lives changed.

There are invisible gifts as we see increased:
- Confidence.
- Influence.
- Clarity.
- Momentum.
- Creativity.

Ideas and stories are powerful and transformative.

As we surrender our lives to God and the writing process, we become a part of this transformation: first, for ourselves and second, for our readers.

When we write, we can step into a close communion with God and allow His creativity to flow through us and into the world.

Are you ready? To begin the journey of writing *with* God and to trust Him with your words, creativity, ministry, and career?

He is the best teacher. He is wisdom and eloquence itself. He desires to guide you every step of the way — as you practice, read, learn, grow, connect to others, and serve.

The writing journey does not have to be lonely or overwhelming.

Instead it can be a deeply satisfying journey filled with wonder, surprise, growth, and the camaraderie of God and the people He brings into your life.

CONCLUSION

If this book has encouraged you, please leave a review on Amazon.com. Each review increases the publicity of this book and message. The world is in desperate need of a revolution of writers, artists and speakers dedicated to serving a higher purpose.

If you are ready to join an online writing group whose members are committed to one another's success, go to: **http://www.facebook.com/groups/unstoppablewriters**

If you have questions or feedback, I love hearing from you. Simply email **welshdeanne@gmail.com**

This book is a physical reminder of God's calling and a few of the lessons He has taught me since I said "yes" to his call to write when I was twelve years old.

It has been over twenty years of wandering through various vocations since then. Each position has been a stepping stone for writing and speaking full time. God has taught me to trust Him with my writing. He is my mentor and muse. I work with writers ready to take the next step and strategically increase their impact and income. You can find me at **www.DeanneWelsh.com** or on Facebook at **http://www.facebook.com/deannewelshwrites**.

Resources

Living with Dragons: Break Free from the Lies Holding You Back by Deanne Welsh

He Whispers: Poetic talks with God, volumes 1-3, by Anne Peterson

Made in the USA
Columbia, SC
19 June 2021